Cinderella

A Family Pantomime

Guy Unsworth

Cinderella © 2021 Guy Unsworth

ISBN 978-1-8380608-4-8

Stuart Jade Publishing
3 Gainsborough Road
Southport
PR8 2EY

Author's Note

A great pantomime feels live, local and up to date. Therefore, a license to perform this comes with full permission for you to tailor it to your own production and audience. Have fun!

Character List

CINDERELLA
Thick skinned, generous, friendly, spirited, heart of gold.
Makes the most of what she's got, and sees the best in all.

BUTTONS
Silly, sweet, charming, cheeky, funny, low self esteem,
Cinderella's best friend.

CHLORINE
Vain, class-aspiring, vicious, acerbic, aggressively sexual,
sharp. Witty, dry, bright. Exceptionally jealous and bitter.

MAUREEN
Fun, dim, curvaceous, copies her sister's example but
ultimately not a bad bone in her body. Low self esteem but
covers it with confidence around men. Probably hides
chocolate bars in her socks.

FAIRY LIQUID
Self-employed, ambitious, freelance Fairy, trying to do good
against everything the world throws against her. Aside from
the magic, she's one of us.

PRINCE CHARMING
Charming, warm, generous. A leader but also a man of the
people. Inexperienced at dating.

DANDINI
Efficient, immaculate, cool, talented, witty, bright, fun, slick,
cheeky but a professional. Closest friend of Prince Charming.

An optional **ENSEMBLE** of villagers, fairies and mummies etc.

* Casting is encouraged to be flexible and imaginative *

Scene List

ACT ONE

ACT TWO

ACT ONE

Scene 0 - The Prologue (front cloth)

VOICEOVER
Ladies and Gentlemen, Boys and Girls, welcome to
'Cinderella'. Please note that the taking of photos and videos
is not allowed, and that this theatre is fitted with ejector
seats, which are triggered automatically at the sound of a
mobile phone or sweet wrapper.

>*Drum roll.*

But now, get ready, boys and girls,
It's time to start the fun.
Panto begins at the [Chelmsford Civic],
in 5, 4, 3, 2, 1!

SONG: Overture

>*FAIRY LIQUID enters.*

FAIRY LIQUID
Hello everybody, my name is Fairy Liquid. I am a self-
confessed, self-employed, self-helping Fairy and I have just
landed the contract of a lifetime - to look after you lot and the
great sun-kissed city of [Chelmsford]. However, pals, not all is
hunky dory here these days.

No, tucked away at Hard Up hall,
Way downstairs in the cellar,
There lives a girl with a heart of gold,
Her name is Cinderella.

>*CINDERELLA is lit through gauze.*

Cinders sees the best in people,

1

Even her two sisters,
But they've been getting worse of late,
Like too big nasty blisters.

SFX distant cackling.

So I've been sent to sort things out,
By the panto committee you see.
Without me her life will never improve,
Like [Chelmsford City] F.C.

But now, sit back, you lovely lot,
It's a special time of year
Our story's titled 'Cinderella'
Come on - let's hear you cheer.

Full bleed through. Cloth out.

Scene 1 - The Village Square (full stage)

SONG: Welcoming everyone to the village.
  (Cinderella and Ensemble)

CINDERELLA
Hello everybody! **(Hello)** I said hello everybody! **(Hello)** My name, is Cinderella, and I live up the road at Hardup Hall with best friend Buttons, and my two sisters. My sisters make my life a little tricky sometimes, but they're lovely really.

VILLAGER 1
Lovely?! Your sisters are wicked, Cinderella.

VILLAGER 2
And they're really horrible to you.

CINDERELLA
They're not *that* bad, are they?

VILLAGER 4
Yes. Last week they made my cat go woof!

CINDERELLA
Well I don't believe that, a cat can't go woof.

VILLAGER 4
It did when they set fire to it. Woof!

CINDERELLA
Oh dear. Did they apologise?

VILLAGER 4
Well, they sent me an identical one to replace it. Now I have *two* dead cats.

VILLAGER 5

Why don't you *leave* Hardup Hall, Cinders?

CINDERELLA
Oh I couldn't do that. When my father died, I promised I'd
look after it for him. And besides, I have my best friend
Buttons to keep me company.

VILLAGER 3
But you need to watch out. Your sisters have been getting
even worse lately.

CINDERELLA
Oh I'll be all right. Besides, you lot'll stick by me won't you?

CHLORINE & MAUREEN (OFF)
Cinderella!!!

VILLAGER 1
Quick everyone, hide! Sorry Cinders, see you later!

VILLAGERS exit. CHLORINE & MAUREEN enter.

CHLORINE & MAUREEN
Hello [Chelmsford]!!

CHLORINE
My name's Chlorine.

MAUREEN
My name's Maureen.

CHLORINE & MAUREEN
And aren't we gorgeous? **(No!)**

CHLORINE
What?! How dare you. You can't talk - It looks like freak night
at Madame Tussauds.

4

MAUREEN
You've come from all 4 corners of the job centre.

CHLORINE
Greggs must have shut early.

CINDERELLA
Don't worry Chlorine and Maureen. These are my new friends!

CHLORINE
Oh look who it is boys and girls.

CHLORINE & MAUREEN
Cinderella!

CHLORINE
Isn't she ugly? **(No!)**

CHLORINE & MAUREEN
Oh yes she is! **(Oh no she isn't!)** Oh yes she is! **(Oh no she isn't!)** Is! Is! Is! **(Isn't! Isn't! Isn't!).**

MAUREEN
Alright don't peak too early.

CHLORINE
Cinderella, you're so ugly your birth certificate was an apology letter. You're so ugly, whenever you go to a haunted house, you come out with a job offer.

MAUREEN
Yeah, you're so ugly you look like a man in a dress.

CINDERELLA
Why do you hate me so much?

CHLORINE

We hate you because you're the spitting image of our mother's late second husband's first wife whom he loved more than he loved our mother.

CHLORINE

MAUREEN
It's complicated but it hangs together psychologically.

CHLORINE
Now run home, Cinderella, and scrub the walls, the floors, the windows and doors. Go!

    CINDERELLA exits.

  (Calling after her)
And don't forget to put the cat out.

MAUREEN
I didn't know it was on fire.

CHLORINE
You are the stupidest thing I've ever known.

MAUREEN
Yesterday you said I was the most *disgusting* thing you've ever known.

CHLORINE
You're that too. There are 5 fat people in this city and you're 4 of them. I've told you before, don't eat anything fatty.

MAUREEN
I had a salad for lunch.

CHLORINE
Still, don't eat *anything,* fatty.

MAUREEN

It's not easy. I rang up weight watchers yesterday and I said 'it's an emergency, can you send somebody round?' They said yes we've got loads of them.

CHLORINE
I told you to eat all the supplements you could find.

MAUREEN
Yes but I nearly choked on part of the Sunday Times.

CHLORINE
Do you know what we both need Maureen?

CHLORINE & MAUREEN
A man!

> *Sexy funk underscore. House lights up. CHLORINE and MAUREEN head into the audience.*

MAUREEN
Oh Chlor, I can smell the testosterone. It's like being in [local shopping centre] on Christmas Eve.

CHLORINE
   (to another man)
Hello tiger, you can meet me round the bike sheds at 12:59 because I'll enjoy that one-to-one time.

MAUREEN
   (to one man)
Hello cupcake, I think you better go to the doctor, 'cause you're lacking some Vitamin Me.

CHLORINE
Oh Chlorine, this man reminds me of the sea.

MAUREEN
What, rough on top but smooth and calm underneath?

CHLORINE
No he makes me feel sick.

MAUREEN
I've never seen so many petrified men.

CHLORINE
Don't worry gentlemen, you can all relax...

CHLORINE & MAUREEN
Apart from you!

MAUREEN
What's your name hunky-monkey? (**Nigel**).

CHLORINE
Ooh [Nigel], what a... heroic name, [Nigel]. Where are you from [Nigel]? (**Romford)**. I'm sorry? (**Romford**). No I heard you the first time I'm just sorry.

CHLORINE
Go on [Nigel], who do you fancy more? Chlorine or Maureen?

CHLORINE
Do you want Claw...aww...aww?

MAUREEN
Or do you want Maur Maur MORE?

CHLORINE & MAUREEN
There's only one right answer.

CHLORINE
You fancy *both* of us?!

MAUREEN
Oh [Nigel] quite the smooth talker.

8

CHLORINE
(Handing him a key)
I tell you what [Nigel], we're going to give you the special key
to our hearts. *(A whisper)* It's actually a key to the cellar,
otherwise known as 'The Detention Room'.

They head back on stage.

MAUREEN
And every time we come on we're going to say:

CHLORINE & MAUREEN
'Who's got the key?'

MAUREEN
And [Nigel], you are going to jump up and shout giddily,

CHLORINE & MAUREEN
'I've got the key, I've got the key!'

CHLORINE
Can you do that for us, [Nigel]? What's that? Yes but you'd
really like to have a practise? Well go on then, if you insist.
Make it a good one, otherwise you'll have to do it twice.
Ready?

CHlORINE & MAUREEN
Who's got the key?

[NIGEL]
I've got the key, I've got the key!

MAUREEN
Oh give him a round of applause everybody.

CHLORINE
Oh [Nigel], I have a feeling that tonight will be a night -

CHLORINE & MAUREEN
- you will never forget.

SONG: Girls on a night out
(Ugly Sisters & ENSEMBLE)

ENSEMBLE enter.

At end of song...

CHLORINE
Come on everyone, let's go sale/Christmas shopping on [local shopping street].

Playout. *ENSEMBLE, CHLORINE and MAUREEN exit.*

Entrance music

BUTTONS enters.

BUTTONS
    MY NAME'S BUTTONS DOO DOO DOO DOO DOO
    MY NAME'S BUTTONS DOO DOO DOO DOO DOO
    MY NAME'S BUTTONS DOO DOO DOO DOO DOO
    MY NAME'S BUTTONS

Alright kids!! My name's Buttons and I work as a servant with my best friend Cinderella at the nearby Hardup Hall.

I love kids - I used to go to school with a load of them. But I got thrown out of school because I farted in Latin. Most people can't even *speak* Latin. Then I got sacked from my job as a mime artist. I asked was it something I said? They said yes. And then I had to give up my job at the helium factory. Well I wasn't going to let them speak to me like that.

But my Dad said to me, 'Buttons, son, you have to fight fire with fire!'. Which is why I then got thrown out the fire brigade.

My careers advisor said, 'Don't dress for the job you've got, dress for the job you want.' I say he was a careers advisor I later found out he was a bin man dressed up as a careers advisor.

So hey my life's a failure but will you lot cheer me up? (**Yes**) I tell you what you can do. Every time I come on I'm gonna sing... My name's buttons doo doo doo doo doo

But I want you lot to do the 'doo doo doo doo doo' bit. Can you do that for me? (**Yes.**) Can you?? (**Yes**!) Let's give it a go then.

MY NAME'S BUTTONS (**DOO DOO DOO DOO DOO**)

Did you do it? I think you can do better than that. Come on, as loud as you can, let's try it again.

MY NAME'S BUTTONS (**DOO DOO DOO DOO DOO**)

That's awesome, you can definitely be my friends! *(An idea!)* 'Ere do you wanna know a secret? (**Yes.**) Alright lean forward, lean forward. Don't worry upstairs, we've only had 2 casualties so far. *(Whispering)* Guess what? (**What?**) I said guess what? (**What?**) I'm in lurrrrve (**Oooh**). With Cinderella (**Oooh!**). But I don't know if she loves me back. *(Pointing at his back)* Not whether she loves my back, but whether my love is precipitated. And every time I try and tell her, something goes horribly wrong. I get down on one knee and I say 'Roses are Red, Violets are Blue, guess what Cinderella?'

CINDERELLA
    (Entering)
What Buttons?

BUTTONS

IIII've done a poo.

CINDERELLA
Excuse me?!

BUTTONS
I mean I *love* poo.

CINDERELLA
Buttons?!

BUTTONS
You.

CINDERELLA
Me?

BUTTONS
You love poo.

CINDERELLA
What??!

BUTTONS
Sorry - Stop.
Stop stop sorry.
Sorry sorry stop stop.
Stop stop sorry.
STOP RIGHT NOW THANK YOU VERY MUCH.
SORRY SEEMS TO BE THE HARDEST -

CINDERELLA
Buttons!

BUTTONS
Sorry

12

CINDERELLA
Did you call me, Buttons?

BUTTONS
No, I called you Cinders.

CINDERELLA
Guess what, Buttons, I've just read on the [Visit Chelmsford] website that Prince Charming of [Romford] is holding a Royal Ball this evening.

CINDERELLA & BUTTONS
        (Star prize moment with audience)
Ooooohhh.

CINDERELLA
How amazing is that?

BUTTONS
That is amazing. And apparently his balls get bigger every year.

        CHLORINE and MAUREEN enter.

Entrance music

CHLORINE & MAUREEN
Aren't we gorgeous? **(No)** Who's got the key? **(I've got the key, I've got the key).**

CHLORINE
What do *you* say, Buttons, aren't I gorgeous?

BUTTONS
If I cover my good eye, you've never looked better.

MAUREEN
        (With Cinderella directly behind her)

And what about me, Buttons, aren't *I* gorgeous?

BUTTONS
Behind every fat woman is a beautiful girl.

CHLORINE
Now I'm glad you're here, Buttons - would you take this
parcel to the post office for me please?

> CHLORINE hands over a parcel (a tin of clattering pieces
> of metal/china indestructibly wrapped in brown paper
> and parcel tape).

BUTTONS
Yes, what is it?

CHLORINE
It's a (/belated) Christmas present for someone very special.

BUTTONS
Ooh. What's the present?

CHLORINE
It's a 24 piece dinner service.

BUTTONS
A 24 piece dinner service? What's it made of?

CHLORINE
Very very fragile, very very expensive, hand carved china.

BUTTONS
Ooh don't send it by post.

MAUREEN
Don't send it by post?

CHLORINE
But why not?

BUTTONS
Well, I'll tell you...

When a parcel goes by post, the postman takes it from the post office and drops it into his sack *(BUTTONS takes the parcel and drops it on the floor)*. Then when he's filled up his sack he throws it over his shoulder *(he picks up the parcel and throws it over his shoulder)* Then at the sorting office they stamp it *(he picks it up and bashes it)* and throw it into another sack *(he throws it on the floor)* but only then can it finally be delivered *(hands over parcel to CHLORINE)*.

So I wouldn't send it by post. What did you say it was again?

CHLORINE
A 48 piece dinner service. I think I'll send it by airmail.

BUTTONS
Oh I wouldn't send it by airmail.

CHLORINE
Why not?

BUTTONS
Well, I'll tell you.

When a parcel goes by airmail, the luggage man takes it and throws it on to the plane *(throws parcel to the side)*. Then as the plane is flying it goes through some turbulence and the parcel gets shaken around *(picks up parcel and shakes it from side to side)*. Then when it gets to the other end the luggage man in the plane throws it to the man on the ground *(he throws the parcel from high up to the floor)* but only then can it finally be delivered *(hands over parcel to CHLORINE)*.

So I wouldn't send it by airmail either. What did you say it was again?

CHLORINE
A 96 piece dinner service. I think I'll send it by boat.

BUTTONS
Oh I wouldn't send it by boat.

CHLORINE
I don't know why not but I bet you're going to tell me.

BUTTONS
I certainly am.

When a parcel goes by boat, the man on the shore throws it to the man on the boat *(he throws it to MAUREEN who catches it)* But the man on the boat drops it *(he knocks it out of her hands and on to MAUREEN's foot)*.

MAUREEN
Agh!

BUTTONS
On to his foot.

MAUREEN
Ooh!

BUTTONS
He's so annoyed -

MAUREEN
     (Covered by SFX beep)
- F*%$ -

BUTTONS

16

- he kicks it away. *(MAUREEN kicks it away)* So another man picks it up and carries it over to the hold but on the way he trips over a rope and drops it *(BUTTONS does trip and drops parcel)*.

CHLORINE
I thought he might.

BUTTONS
Then he throws it up to the ship's boatswain *(BUTTONS throws it up to CINDERELLA)*. The boatswain throws it up to the captain *(CINDERELLA throws it to BUTTONS)*. The captain throws it over to the Cocktail pianist *(BUTTONS throws it to MD who catches it whilst playing)* and the pianist throws it back to the man on the dock *(MD throws it back to BUTTONS)* but only then can it finally be delivered *(hands over parcel to CHLORINE)*.

So I wouldn't send it by boat. What did you say it was again?

CHLORINE
A 700 piece dinner service.

BUTTONS
Well if it's a fragile thing like that, why don't you deliver it personally?

CHLORINE
I think that's a good idea.

She hands it to him.

Happy Christmas, Buttons.

Musical tag.

CINDERELLA

Hey girls, have you heard? Prince Charming of [Romford] is holding a big party this evening!

CHLORINE
Prince Charming of Romford!

MAUREEN
Famous for his balls?

CINDERELLA
That's right! He's inviting all the eligible maidens.

CHLORINE
Maureen, we're off to a party.

CINDERELLA
I'm hoping to be invited too.

CHLORINE
You?! Oh no you're far too ugly!

BUTTONS
Hey! She's my friend. Say you're sorry!

CHLORINE
I'm sorry she's your friend. *(To CINDERELLA)* Go and fetch us some firewood, Cinderella, I want a hot bath later. Come on Maureen, we need to find an escort for tonight.

MAUREEN
  (Exiting behind CHLORINE)
I saw one on the road outside the theatre.

BUTTONS
Oh Cinders, I hate it when they speak to you like that, especially Chlorine.

CINDERELLA
Ah well, sticks and stones may break my bones but words will never hurt me.

BUTTONS
I used to think that until I fell into a printing press.

CINDERELLA
(looking up)
If my father was still here, he'd tell me to stand strong and ignore them.

BUTTONS
Yeah. I know wherever *my* Dad is he's always looking down on me. He's not dead, just very condescending.

Music in.

CINDERELLA
I can always count on you to lighten the mood, Buttons!

BUTTONS
I'm not your only friend though Cinders, *(to offstage)* am I guys?!

Ensemble join.

**SONG Having fun together
(BUTTONS, CINDERS, and ENSEMBLE)**

Cloth in. **Tag.**

Scene 2 - Edge of the Forest (front cloth)

FAIRY LIQUID
Hello [Chelmsford] chums, are you having fun? **(Yes!)** That's great! Cinderella's rising above her sisters' wicked ways, but things are soon going to get a bit complicated. The next time you see me, I'll be in disguise. Before that, I've a story for you.

> *Musical flourish, as the ensemble rush in and form a line holding very large white cards with logos on. With the following slogans, FAIRY LIQUID points to the respective logos (listed below).*

You see I've not always been a fairy. You're probably thinking '**Maybe She's Born With It?**'. But no.

One day at work, I thought I'd **Have a Break,** when this bloke walked past and whistled at me (***Macdonald's whistle***). Now some don't mind being whistled at, and **8 Out Of 10 Cats *Prefer* It**, but then he said 'Eugh - **I Should Have Gone To Specsaver**, you're not **The Best A Man Can Get!**'. Maybe that's his way to **Per per per Pick up a** woman, but I thought **Ch Ch Ch Charmin!**

Maybelline, Kit Kat, McDonald's, Whiskers, Specsaver, Gilette, Penguin, Charmin.

At first I said **'Have it your way'** but '**There is more than one way to slice it.**' C'mon! I need to **Think Big. This isn't just *any*** whistle. **Wasssuuup** with the world? I can't live long with this **King of Beers**. ***Washing Machines*** Live **Longer With *Calgon.***

Burger King, Spam, Vauxhall Corsa, Imax, M&S, Budweiser, Budweiser, Calgon.

Now I know **Good Things Come To Those Who Wait** but I

thought the **Holidays Are Coming**, I need to **Just Do it** and become a qualified fairy. The **Creative Technologie** sometimes makes you **Think Different**, it even **Gives you Wiiiings** and you need to **Love The Skin You're In** but **What's The Worst That Can Happen**?

Guinness, Coca Cola, Nike, Citroen, Apple, Red Bull, Olay, Dr Pepper.

And now as a qualified fairy I'm bringing the **Power To You** to **Believe in Better. Success? It's a Mind Game.** I **Zoom Zoom** around the place and **Snap Crackle and Pop** anything in my way: **Styling the Nation, Connecting People, Making Everyday More Comfortable. If Carlsberg made fairies they'd probably be the best fairies in the world** but **This Is Living.** I want to **Have a Happy Period** in life - and now my smile is the **Number 1 Recommended By Dentists** (*Musical Ting*). In short, this fairy **Won't Let You Down** and **That's Why Mums Go To Me** because **there are some things money can't buy** - it's **Simples - I am what I am** and **I do Exactly What It Says On The Tin - You Either Love it Or You Hate It** but **The Future's Bright,** and ever since all that (***MacDonald's whistle***) **I'm loving it!**

Vodafone, Sky, Tag Heuer, Mazda, Rice Crispies, Debenhams, Nokia, DFS, Carlsberg, Playstation 3, Always, Colgate, Iceland, Mastercard, Compare the Market, Reebok, Ronseal, Marmite, Orange, Macdonald's.

Ensemble exit except one who remains, holding a blank card.

We were going to print them on individual cards, but then we discovered (*turning over card to reveal one big Plenty logo*) **'One Sheet Does Plenty'.**

Musical tag as FAIRY GODMOTHER and ENSEMBLE member exits.

PRINCE CHARMING and DANDINI enter.

PRINCE CHARMING
Come on then Dandini, if I'm hosting a Royal Ball tonight, we must deliver the invites before it's too late.

DANDINI
Prince Charming, your father insists you find a suitable bride at the Ball, so I've found the very best in [Essex]. There's a girl called Grace with a gorgeous face. A lady named Clare with perfect hair. And then there's Rose with a lovely nose. Or even Annie and her fantastic personality.

PRINCE CHARMING
I get the picture - but how can I be sure they're interested in *who* I am not *what* I am. I hate holding parties, the girls who attend only want my money, or a title.

DANDINI
If I were a Prince, I'd have parties every night and a royal ball every other week.

PRINCE CHARMING
Are you criticising me?

DANDINI
No, before I criticise a man, I like to walk a mile in his shoes. That way when I *do* criticise him, I'm a mile away and I have his shoes.

PRINCE CHARMING
I know, let's swap identities, just until the Ball tonight. If you take the Royal sash, I bet no one will even notice. What do you say? You be me and I'll be you.

Music in. PRINCE CHARMING hands DANDINI his sash.

After the first verse, DANDINI shouts 'Guards' and the ENSEMBLE enter as GUARDS.

**SONG: Disguise / Let the games begin
(Prince, Dandini & Ensemble)**

PRINCE CHARMING
Well then, 'Prince Charming', have a good afternoon, sir! I'm a free man for the next few hours.

DANDINI
A free man you say? I don't think so. You need to deliver these invites. I'm the free man. See you later, Dandini!

They all exit in opposite directions.

***Tag**, as the cloth flies out.*

Scene 3 - The Enchanted Forest (front cloth)

CINDERELLA
Hello boys and girls. I've just managed to find some firewood before it gets dark. At least my sisters can have their hot bath now.

FAIRY LIQUID enters in disguise as an old lady.

FAIRY LIQUID
(Scottish accent)
Alms for the poor. Alms for the poor.

CINDERELLA
Hello there. I'm afraid I don't have any coins I can give you.

FAIRY LIQUID
Credit Cards for the poor. Credit cards for the poor.

CINDERELLA
I'm afraid I don't have a credit card either.

FAIRY LIQUID
Branches for the poor. Branches for the poor.

CINDERELLA
Branches yes! There are some off in that direction. Oh but it's getting dark and it'll be very dangerous for you. Look, take mine, I'm sure I will find some on my way home.

FAIRY LIQUID
Are you sure?

CINDERELLA
Please.

FAIRY LIQUID
Dear, dear, I'd offer you a sweetie, sweetie, but I've an empty pocket, poppet. Still, I will return this kindness when you need it most.

FAIRY LIQUID starts to exit.

CINDERELLA
When I need it most?

FAIRY LIQUID
In the meantime, luck will come when you least expect it. Goodbye Cinderella.

FAIRY LIQUID is gone.

CINDERELLA
Goodbye! But wait, how do you know my name? *(To herself)* That's strange!

CHLORINE (OFF)
This way Maureen - quickly!

CINDERELLA
Oh no. It's my sisters. I better get going. See you later everyone.

CINDERELLA runs off. CHLORINE and MAUREEN enter.

Entrance music

CHLORINE & MAUREEN
Aren't we gorgeous? **(No!)** Who's got the key? **(I've got the key, I've got the key).**

CHLORINE
Look Maureen, there's a man coming. Be polite and gentile, we are demure ladies of society.

MAUREEN
Demure ladies of society.

DANDINI enters and passes by them.

DANDINI
Good afternoon, Gentlemen.

CHLORINE & MAUREEN
(manly and rude)
EXCUUUUUUUSE ME!

CHLORINE
Good Afternoon Gentlemen?!?! Correct yourself young man!

DANDINI
Oh, I'm terribly sorry. Good *Evening*, Gentlemen.

CHLORINE & MAUREEN
WAIT A MINUUUUUUTE!

CHLORINE
Do you know what we are??! We are ladies!

MAUREEN
Looking for men!

CHLORINE
At least call me Madam - idiot.

DANDINI
Sorry, Madam idiot. I am Dan- er - Prince Charming.

CHLORINE
What? Not *the* Prince Charming?

MAUREEN

Famous for his balls?

DANDINI
That's right.

CHLORINE
Well why didn't you say? Introduce me, Maureen.

Drum roll.

MAUREEN
Your Royal Majesticals, this is my older twin sister Chlorine.
She is Posh with a capital OSH. She's so up-market the boss
of Tesco said she could be his bag for life.

*Cue 4 bars of high energy drum music. CHLORINE
crosses the stage to DANDINI throwing outrageously
sexual moves, impressively and aggressively.*

Blimey, Chlorine. Can you teach me to do all that stuff with
your legs?

CHLORINE
How flexible are you?

MAUREEN
I can do Tuesdays.

CHLORINE
You don't need me, Maureen, just believe in yourself. Besides
I've had music written specially for you.

MAUREEN
All right, introduce me.

Drum roll.

CHLORINE
Your Royal Detergent, this is my younger twin sister Maureen.
She is FAT with a capital FAT. In fact she's so fat her blood
type is Ragu.

> *Cue 4 bars of cacophonous out of time/tune music as*
> *MAUREEN attempts to move sexually to it. Finally she*
> *bends over followed by SFX of a fart. She is panting in*
> *short breaths.*

MAUREEN
I think I'm having a heart attack.

DANDINI
Big Breaths madam.

MAUREEN
   (Sticks her chest out, still with short pants)
Why thank you but I think I'm having a heart attack. How
about a little smooch, Princey? I have everything a man
desires.

CHLORINE
Big thighs and a hairy moustache?

MAUREEN
Oh!

DANDINI
I really must be going.

CHLORINE
What about *me* Princey? Men say I'm a lovely kisser.

MAUREEN
Yeah. She used to syphon petrol out of army lorries.

DANDINI

Not today ladies.

CHLORINE
Come on, close your eyes, let's you and I have a quick round
of tongue wrestling.

> From either side and with their eyes closed, CHLORINE
> and MAUREEN move slowly closer to DANDINI, their
> lips puckered.

MAUREEN
A little match a tonsil tennis.

CHLORINE
A game of sucky-sucky face.

MAUREEN
A set of Saliva swapsies.

CHLORINE & MAUREEN
Here, I, come.

> DANDINI, horrified, ducks out of the way causing
> MAUREEN and CHLORINE to kiss each other on the lips
> (SFX kiss). They see each other.

CHLORINE & MAUREEN
Aaaagggghhhhhh!

DANDINI
Ladies. You deserve *better* than me.

CHLORINE & MAUREEN
But you're gorgeous!

DANDINI
In that case *I* deserve better than *you*. Bye.

DANDINI exits.

CHLORINE & MAUREEN
Princey! Wait!

CHLORINE and MAUREEN chase him off.

Short tag. Cloth in.

Scene 4 - Edge of the Forest (front cloth)

CINDERELLA enters.

CINDERELLA
'I will return this kindness when you need it most'. What a strange thing to say! *And* she knew my name! Still, I like the idea of luck coming my way when I least expect it.

PRINCE CHARMING crosses.

PRINCE CHARMING
Hello.

CINDERELLA
Hello.

Musical ting. They stop.

PRINCE CHARMING
Do I know you?

CINDERELLA
/Do I know you?

PRINCE CHARMING
Sorry, you go first.

CINDERELLA
/Sorry, you go first.

PRINCE CHARMING
No please - after you.

CINDERELLA
/No please - after you.

CINDERELLA
Nice to meet you, I'm...erm...sorry I'm tongue tied.

PRINCE CHARMING
That's a funny name, but no need to apologise. I'm Prince Charming...'s servant, Dandini.

CINDERELLA
Not *The* Prince Charming?

PRINCE CHARMING
His servant yes.

CINDERELLA
I've always wanted to meet the Prince.

PRINCE CHARMING
You could meet him at the Royal Ball.

CINDERELLA
Oh, I'm not invited.

PRINCE CHARMING
You could come as my guest. Here.

   He gives her an invitation.

CINDERELLA
Oh I'd love to, but I've nothing to wear.

PRINCE CHARMING
Come exactly as you are - it's very... shabby-chique.

CINDERELLA
Thank you, but I'm sure the prince wouldn't approve.

PRINCE CHARMING

Leave it with me, I think he's persuadable.

SONG: Pop, playful, young-love duet.
   (Cinderella and Prince charming)

CHLORINE (off)
Princeypots!!

MAUREEN (off)
Where are you??

CINDERELLA
Oh I can't be seen with you. I must run. Thank you for the invite.

     CINDERELLA exits.

PRINCE CHARMING
But wait, I don't know your name.

     DANDINI enters.

DANDINI
I need your help.

PRINCE CHARMING
There you are Dandini. The most amazing thing's just happened.

CHLORINE & MAUREEN (off)
Princeypie!

DANDINI
Quick, hold your cloak up.

PRINCE CHARMING
What?

DANDINI
Just do it!

> *DANDINI lifts PRINCE CHARMING's hands up so that his cloak conceals DANDINI.*

CHLORINE
Where did he go?

PRINCE CHARMING
Who?

CHLORINE
Prince Charming of course.

PRINCE CHARMING
Prince Charming?

MAUREEN
Famous for his balls!

PRINCE CHARMING
But *I* am Pri - *(DANDINI nudges him)* oooh - He went that way *(they run after him)* but he can't stop.

CHLORINE
How do you know?

PRINCE CHARMING
I work for him. I am Dandini.

MAUREEN
Houdini?

PRINCE CHARMING
Dandini!

MAUREEN
Martini?

PRINCE CHARMING
Dandini!!

MAUREEN
Bikini?

PRINCE CHARMING
Dandini!!! I am an equerry.

CHLORINE
We don't care *what* your star sign is. Give us those
invitations.

> She snatches the invites in his hand.

(Exiting)
We'll see you at the palace, and tell the Prince we've got plans
to do naughty things with him.

PRINCE CHARMING
Then you'll get a big surprise.

MAUREEN
Not as big as the surprise he'll get.

> *CHLORINE and MAUREEN exit.*

PRINCE CHARMING
What was all that about?

DANDINI
You're right, the life of a prince is harder than you think.

PRINCE CHARMING

I told you. Come on, I've got a ball to arrange. And something brilliant to tell you on the way.

DANDINI and PRINCE CHARMING exit.

Tag. *Reveal to...*

Scene 5 - Hardup Hall Kitchen (full stage)

BUTTONS enters.

BUTTONS
    MY NAME'S BUTTONS **(DOO DOO DOO DOO DOO)**

That's brilliant guys! And guess what, I've worked out exactly how to tell Cinders that I love her. This time, I'm gonna get down on one knee, and I'm gonna say 'Cinderella!'

Buttons produces the relevant <u>items</u> below instantaneously.

CINDERELLA
    (Entering)
Yes Buttons?

BUTTONS
Alright fella!

CINDERELLA
I'm sorry?

BUTTONS
Want some <u>Mozzarella</u>?

CINDERELLA
Not really I-

BUTTONS
A <u>classic Novella</u>?

CINDERELLA
Buttons, I-

BUTTONS
Under my <u>Umbrella</u>, ella, ella, eh, eh, eh, eh.

CINDERELLA
Is everything alright, Buttons?

BUTTONS
Sorry Cinders, I forgot myself for a moment.

CINDERELLA
Oh Buttons. I met this wonderful man today who has invited
me as his guest to the Royal Ball.

BUTTONS
You met a man?

CINDERELLA
Yes he was tall, handsome and wonderfully charming.

BUTTONS
Tall? Handsome?

CINDERELLA
And wonderfully charming. His name is Dandini.

BUTTONS
Tall? Handsome?

CINDERELLA
He works for Prince Charming.

BUTTONS
Tall? Handsome?

CINDERELLA
Isn't that brilliant?

BUTTONS
It's a knock out.

CINDERELLA
Aren't you happy for me?

BUTTONS
Ecstatic.

CHLORINE AND MAUREEN enter.

CHLORINE & MAUREEN
ALL THE SINGLE LADIES, ALL THE SINGLE LADIES,
WE GOT AN INVITE, WE GOT AN INVITE, WE GOT AN INVITE.

CINDERELLA
That's brilliant news - we can go together because I've got an invite too.

CHLORINE
What?! From who?!

CINDERELLA
Dandini. He's an equerry.

CHLORINE
I don't care *what* his star sign is, you're not going to the ball until you've scrubbed the walls, the floors, the windows and doors, and Maureen's dirty crevices.

CINDERELLA
But -

CHLORINE
No! Buts!

CINDERELLA runs off.

MAUREEN
I'm glad you said no buts - I'd rather clean my own.

CHLORINE
Oh Maureen you are so stupid! *(To audience)* Some thieves broke into our house last week and stole the television. Maureen chased after them shouting "Wait, you forgot the remote!"

MAUREEN
Eh don't be mean.

CHLORINE
And yesterday she got run over by a parked car.

MAUREEN
Ah yes but talking of cars, somebody complimented me on my driving today. They left a little note on the windscreen, it said 'Parking Fine.'

BUTTONS
I think you're being mean, Chlorine. Anyway, she's brighter than you.

CHLORINE
Oh no she isn't. **(Oh yes she is.)** Oh no she isn't. **(Oh yes she is.)**

BUTTONS
Then I think we have to settle this via a Quiz. 10 questions each, the contestant who wins the quiz is the least stupid. Chlorine, happy?

CHLORINE
Happy.

BUTTONS
Maureen happy?

MAUREEN
What's a quiz?

BUTTONS
Excellent. Maureen you can go first. Good luck, let's play...

Dramatic lights and SFX cheesy jingle plays 'WHO IS THE STUPIDEST OF THEM ALL?'

Question 1. What is the capital city of England?

MAUREEN
Erm, an orangutan!

BUTTONS
Incorrect. The answer is London. Question 2, what is 5 multiplied by 5?

MAUREEN
An orangutan!

BUTTONS
No, 25. Now this is easier, Maureen, what colour is a pink elephant?

MAUREEN
Grey!

BUTTONS
I tell you what, Maureen, if you don't know the answer just say pass.

MAUREEN
Right.

BUTTONS
Question 4, What is a narrow pathway between two mountains?

MAUREEN
Pass.

BUTTONS
Correct. When you succeed in an examination, you what?

MAUREEN
Pass.

BUTTONS
Correct. In football -

MAUREEN
Pass.

BUTTONS
Correct. In tennis -

CHLORINE
(bursting)
Ohhhh you cannot be serious!

BUTTONS
Yes, that is correct!!

MAUREEN
Thanks Chlor.

BUTTONS
What is a red herring?

MAUREEN
Not a clue.

BUTTONS
Correct. What do you call a blind Bambi?

MAUREEN
No idea.

BUTTONS
Correct. What do you call a blind Bambi with no legs?

MAUREEN
Still no idea.

BUTTONS
Correct. And a free bonus question, Maureen - you may as
well have a guess - if you looked at yourself in a mirror, what
would you see?

MAUREEN
An orangutan?

BUTTONS
Correct. You scored 8 points!

> *Musical 'Tada'. Lights revert.*

CHLORINE
That's ridiculous, those questions were rigged.

BUTTONS
They were checked by my independent adjudicator [Nigel].
Now then Chlorine, you have 8 points to beat. Good luck, let's
play...

> *Dramatic lights and SFX jingle plays 'WHO IS THE
> STUPIDEST OF THEM ALL?'*

BUTTONS
What is the capital of France?

CHLORINE
Easy - Paris.

BUTTONS

Correct. What is 12 multiplied by 6?

CHLORINE
72.

BUTTONS
Correct. What is Maureen as daft as?

CHLORINE
An orangutan.

BUTTONS
Correct. True or false, a kangaroo can jump higher than the Empire State Building.

CHLORINE
False.

BUTTONS
No it's true. The Empire State Building can't jump. Question 5, what time is it when the clock strikes 13?

CHLORINE
One o'clock!

BUTTONS
No, it's time to get a new clock. What would you have if you put a *yellow* hat in the *Red* sea?

CHLORINE
An orange hat.

BUTTONS
No, you'd have a wet hat. If a blue house is made of blue bricks, and a purple house is made of purple bricks, what is a green house made of?

CHLORINE
Green bricks.

BUTTONS
No it's made of glass. What country's capital city is the fastest
growing in the world?

CHLORINE
Errm, China?

BUTTONS
No the answer is Ireland. Every year it's Dublin. What do you
do if you see a spaceman?

CHLORINE
I don't know.

BUTTONS
Park your car in it, man. Final question: why do you, Chlorine,
never go to the toilet in a pub?

CHLORINE
The urinals are always dirty *(shocked at her admission)* AH!

> *Musical Tada. Lights revert.*

BUTTONS
Correct, but I'm afraid, Chlorine, you only scored 4 points,
and that means...

> *SFX jingle plays 'CHLORINE's THE STUPIDEST OF THEM
> ALL'*

CHLORINE
It's a fix, you rigged it.

BUTTONS

But the proof is in the pudding.

> *SFX jingle plays 'CHLORINE's THE STUPIDEST OF THEM ALL'*

CHLORINE
I hate losing.

BUTTONS
If you hate losing it must be hard to know that...

> *SFX jingle plays 'CHLORINE's THE STUPIDEST OF THEM ALL'*

CHLORINE
Stop it! Stop it! Stop it! *(To Buttons)* I'm not stupider than *you*.

BUTTONS
   (And audience)
Oh yes you are!

CHLORINE
Oh no I'm not!

BUTTONS & MAUREEN
   (And audience)
Oh yes you are!

CHLORINE
Oh no I'm not!

BUTTONS
Then we'll have to settle it once and for all. Maureen you can ask the questions and I'll answer them *(Hands her a Qs card)*. Good luck to me, as I play...

Dramatic lights and SFX jingle plays 'WHO IS THE STUPIDEST OF THEM ALL?'

MAUREEN
Question 1. What is orange and sounds like a parrot?

BUTTONS
Err... a carrot.

MAUREEN
Correct. What dogs do magicians have?

BUTTONS
Labracadabradors.

MAUREEN
Correct. What dinosaur is blind?

BUTTONS
Doyouthinkhesaurus.

MAUREEN
And why can't dinosaurs go disco dancing?

BUTTONS
They're extinct.

MAUREEN
What do you call Postman Pat when he's on holiday?

BUTTONS
Pat.

MAUREEN
If I had 6 apples in one hand, and 12 in the other, what would I have?

BUTTONS
Very large hands.

MAUREEN
Correct, and for maximum points, if I gave you two bars of chocolate and I take one away, how many would you have?

BUTTONS
Two.

MAUREEN
Correct, ten points!

    Musical 'Tada'.

CHLORINE
Wait wait wait wait wait!! That's *in*correct, you'd have *one* chocolate bar.

BUTTONS
I'd have *two*.

CHLORINE
You'd have *one*!

BUTTONS
If Maureen gave me two bars of chocolate and took one away, I'd have two.

CHLORINE
No, you'd have one.

BUTTONS
I'd have two.

CHLORINE
You'd have one!

BUTTONS
What do *you* think Maureen, what would I have?

MAUREEN
An orangutan?

CHLORINE
Look, I'll prove it. Maureen, give him two bars of chocolate.

    MAUREEN gives him two bars of chocolate.

MAUREEN
Two bars of chocolate. One, two.

CHLORINE
Now take one away.

MAUREEN
(doing it)
Taking one away.

CHLORINE
And what have you got?

Buttons
Two.

CHLORINE
You've got one!

BUTTONS
I've got two!

CHLORINE
How can you have two?!

BUTTONS
I've got another in my pocket. Wahey!

They chase him off.

SFX jingle plays 'CHLORINE'S THE STUPIDEST OF THEM ALL?'

CINDERELLA enters scrubbing the floors.

**SONG: of hope, love and resilience
  (Cinderella)**

CHLORINE and MAUREEN enter.

CHLORINE
Hello, Cinderella, how are you getting on?

CINDERELLA
All finished, as you requested, Chlorine.

CHLORINE
Oh well done. In that case are you looking forward to the Ball?

CINDERELLA
I can't wait!

CHLORINE
And are you all ready to meet the Prince?

CINDERELLA
As ready as I'll ever be.

CHLORINE
But have you got your invite to present at the Palace gates?

CINDERELLA
   (Holding it up)
I certainly do.

CHLORINE
Oh good. Rip it up.

   Ominous underscore hangs in the air.

CINDERELLA
What?

MAUREEN
Eh?

CHLORINE
I said rip it up.

CINDERELLA
What? Why?!

   Evil underscore kicks in and builds.

CHLORINE & MAUREEN
Rip. It. Up.

   She tears it.

Again!

   She tears it again.

Again!

   She tears it again.

Again!

She tears it again.

CHLORINE
Now pick up the pieces.

Cinders is crying.

CINDERELLA
Why would you do this?

CHLORINE
Don't get upset, Cinderella, it's Christmas time! And you know what happens at Christmas don't you, Maureen?

MAUREEN
What?

CHLORINE
   (Pushing the handful of torn up paper up in the air)
It snows!

   CHLORINE and MAUREEN exit with a cackle. Evil sting.

BUTTONS
   (Entering)
Hey Cinders, there you are, I've been looking all over for you. Knock Knock.

CINDERELLA
Who's there?

Buttons
A little old lady.

CINDERELLA
A little old lady who?

BUTTONS
Wow I didn't know you could yodel.

BUTTONS is laughing. CINDERELLA is crying.

Thought that'd make you laugh.

CINDERELLA
I'm not laughing Buttons, I'm crying.

BUTTONS
It's not *that* funny.

CINDERELLA
Chlorine made me tear up my invitation.

BUTTONS
What?! That's terrible!

CINDERELLA
Now what am I going to do?

BUTTONS
    (*Picking up one of the pieces*)
Maybe if you took this bit they'd let you in for five minutes?

CINDERELLA
I just want to go to the Ball.

BUTTONS
Well we'll have our own ball right here. All you need is a ball gown. (*Buttons takes the table cloth and puts it around her.*) This one's made by the famous fashion designer Annette Curtain.

CINDERELLA
Buttons...

BUTTONS
Come on, don't be so clothes minded. Now you need a gold
necklace. *(He takes a string of carrots and puts it around her
neck)* One gold necklace. That's eighteen carrots. And we
need something to make you look like a princess: Tiara, Tiara,
Tiara... Tiara!!

> *Female ensemble member comes on dressed as a stage
> manager.*

Hi Tiara, do you have anything to make Cinders look like a
princess?

> *She hands him a colander.*

BUTTONS
(Putting a colander on her head)
A colander - perfect - thanks Tiara. There you go - one Royal
Colander. Now the paparazzi have caught you on the red
carpet. Pose for camera. Snap, snap. Snap, snap. There you
go, if you take them to Snappysnaps, someday your prints
will come.

CINDERELLA
Oh Buttons - you are silly.

BUTTONS
You're the one wearing the colander.

> *Music in.*

CINDERELLA
You always know how to cheer me up.

BUTTONS
Well that's what friendship's all about. You see...

SONG Friendship
(CINDERELLA and BUTTONS)

BUTTONS
Hey Cinders, shall we watch that documentary on the key to building ship containers? Apparently it's riveting... Cinders?

CINDERELLA
Oh, Buttons. No matter how much fun we have here, I keep wondering what it must be like at the Palace. I think I need to be alone right now.

BUTTONS
Sorry Cinders. Sure. I understand. I'll be in my room if you need me.

*Buttons starts to exit slowly SR. (**Aaaah**)*

CINDERELLA
Buttons?

BUTTONS
Yeah?

CINDERELLA
Thank you for being my friend.

BUTTONS
Friend? Yeah, no problem.

*Slow exit again SR. (**Aaaah**)*

(To audience)
Don't patronise me.

BUTTONS exits.

SONG Reprise Solo
(CINDERELLA)

SFX Double Knock from SR.

CINDERELLA
Who's there?

FAIRY LIQUID (off)
A little old lady.

CINDERELLA
(Heading to the door SR)
Buttons! Not your yodelling joke again -

FAIRY LIQUID enters.

FAIRY LIQUID
Hello Cinderella.

CINDERELLA
Who are you?

FAIRY LIQUID
I am Fairy Liquid, your Fairy Godmother.

CINDERELLA
My Fairy Godmother?

FAIRY LIQUID
I'm here to protect you and make your dreams come true.

CINDERELLA
But why did you just say you were a little old lady?

FAIRY LIQUID
I thought it might remind you of when you last saw me.

CINDERELLA
When I last saw you?

She drops into her hag pose.

It was you!

FAIRY LIQUID
Yep... I thank you. But now, as promised, I'm returning the kindness when you need it most.

CINDERELLA
Oh I don't need kindness, my best friend Buttons is always kind to me.

FAIRY LIQUID
Buttons *is* kind you're right about that, but you deserve something more. Besides there's someone waiting for you at the palace, who knows what lies in store.

To miss the Ball this evening
Could amount to something tragic,
And haven't you noticed, I'm speaking in rhyme?

CiNDERELLA
Why's that?-

FAIRY LIQUID
              -'Cause it sounds like magic.

Your invitation's on its way,
I got it on Amazon Prime.
They've said that they'll deliver by drone
In fact - now's about time.

An invitation drops from the sky. The following (bracketed) lines can be spoken if she drops it!

CINDERELLA
Wow thank you!

FAIRY LIQUID
Nice one girl, that's quite a catch
(/ Better luck next time Cinderella,)
N' I know (/to be fair) it took you off guard,
Now I need a Pumpkin to make a coach,

CINDERELLA
A pumpkin? There's one in the yard.

CINDERELLA exits to get the pumpkin.

FAIRY LIQUID
But put a cloak on, it's freezing outside
The weather just hasn't improved,
    (To audience)
Even the snowman seems to be cold,
Either that or his carrot's been moved.

CINDERELLA enters wearing a cloak. We clearly see her face before she puts the hood up. With the next instruction she EXITS immediately.

CINDERELLA
One pumpkin, there we are.

FAIRY LIQUID
Last but not least a cage of mice
What for? Only time will tell.
    (Exit CINDERELLA)
And I'll need some friends to help me out,
To weave my magic spell.

The ENSEMBLE enter and transform the set and A DOUBLE OF CINDERELLA returns with the cage of mice.

FAIRY LIQUID and the DOUBLE watch the transformation from downstage...

Scene 6 - Transformation (full stage)

SONG Once Upon A Time Part 1
(Fairy Godmother and ensemble)

> *The DOUBLE OF CINDERELLA is taken into the middle with backlight to cover her face. With mass movement from the ensemble, she swaps with the real CINDERELLA, who is revealed now in her ball gown.*

CINDERELLA
Fairy Liquid, how can I ever thank you?

FAIRY LIQUID
(in prose)
Cinderella, listen carefully. Only the Prince will recognise you, so your sisters won't interfere. However, the spell will only last until midnight.

> *Drum Roll*

(Back in rhythm)
When the clock strikes twelve, real life will restore,
Your transport, dress and all.
Don't forget now Cinders,

CINDERELLA
                              I promise I won't!

FAIRY LIQUID
Then it's time you must go to the ball!

SONG Once Upon A Time Part 2
(Fairy Godmother and ensemble)

> *A coach and ponies enter.*

CINDERELLA is escorted into the coach.

CINDERELLA rides off to the ball.

End of Act One.

ACT TWO

Scene 1 - The Royal Ballroom (full stage)

SONG Welcome to the Ball
   (Dandini and Ensemble)

DANDINI
Ladies and Gentlemen, welcome to the Royal Ball. Drinks are on the house but the barman would like his glasses back at the bar. He can't see a thing without them.

   CHLORINE & MAUREEN enter

Entrance music

CHLORINE & MAUREEN
Aren't we gorgeous? **(No)** Who's got the key? **(I've got the key, I've got the key.)**

CHLORINE
(To Dandini)
Your majesticals! Where have you been all my life?

DANDINI
I don't think I was born for most of it.

CHLORINE
Do you know, I'm wearing my sheepdog bra - rounds 'em up and heads 'em in the right direction.

MAUREEN
And I'm wearing my Donald Trump legal team knickers.

CHLORINE
Covering up a massive ar -

DANDINI
SOOOO good to see you ladies, but there are plenty of eligible bachelors here tonight. Why me when you could have any Tom, Dick or Harry?

MAUREEN
I don't want Tom or Harry.

> The PRINCE enters and talks privately to DANDINI.

PRINCE CHARMING
She's still not arrived. I think we should go ahead and announce dinner.

DANDINI
Very well sir.

CHLORINE
Err excuse me! Interrupting us like that. Who do you think you are?

DANDINI
> (Publicly)
My Lords, Ladies and Gentlemen: Prince Charming.

PRINCE CHARMING
> (Walking nonchalantly past)
Good evening ladies. And a very warm welcome to you all.

MAUREEN
> (Rushing to DANDINI)
Hey. If that's the Prince, who are you?

DANDINI
I am Dandini.

MAUREEN
Zucchini?

DANDINI
Dandini!

MAUREEN
Linguine?

DANDINI
Dandini!!

MAUREEN
The Genie?!

DANDINI
Dandini!!! I am an equerry.

CHLORINE
I don't care *what* your star sign is, now get out of the way.

    (Charmingly, to PRINCE CHARMING)
Your Grace!

MAUREEN
Your Disgrace!

CHLORINE
It is an Honour to meet you. My name's Chlorine but you can call me Chlor.

MAUREEN
And my name's Maureen and you can call me anytime.

CHLORINE
Don't mind her, your principals, she has a strange affliction called butterface.

PRINCE CHARMING
Butterface?

CHLORINE
Everything's fine but her face.

DANDINI
(publicly)
My Lords, Ladies and Gentlemen, please welcome Princess Crystal.

    Music, as CINDERELLA enters.

CHLORINE
    (to Maureen)
Who is that?

MAUREEN
    (to Chlorine)
I don't know.

CHLORINE
I've not seen a dress like that since I took to the stage as Queen Elizabeth I.

MAUREEN
Which really upset the cast of the Lion King.

PRINCE CHARMING
Princess Crystal!

CINDERELLA
Prince Charming!

PRINCE CHARMING
I didn't know you were a Princess.

CINDERELLA
I didn't know you were a Prince.

PRINCE CHARMING
Like your name, you're very beautiful.

CINDERELLA
Like yours, you're very charming.

CHLORINE
Like bungee jumping, you're very sickening. Come on, let's go to the bar. Drinks are on the house apparently.

MAUREEN
I'll go get a ladder.

CHLORINE and MAUREEN exit.

DANDINI
Ladies and Gentlemen, dinner is served in the dining room.

PRINCE CHARMING
If you'll join me on the terrace I can explain everything.

Tag. *Cloth in. The crowd are exiting.*

Scene 2 - Palace Corridor (front cloth)

MAUREEN enters, followed by CHLORINE.

MAUREEN
D'ya know, I reckon the prince gave me the once over.

CHLORINE
Yes he looked once and it was all over. It must be your wrinkles.

MAUREEN
These aren't wrinkles. They're laughter lines.

CHLORINE
Nothing's *that* funny.

MAUREEN
Now don't be mean, I'm not sleeping at the moment.

SONG: WHERE DID YOU GET THAT HAT?
   (Uglies, Buttons, dandini)

This routine is to the tune of the music hall number 'Where did you get that hat?'.

CHLORINE
Not sleeping? Then I have the answer to all your troubles. *(Grabbing a hat from the wings. It has a Japanese pattern on it)* This is a magic hat. Father gave it to me.

MAUREEN
Very nice! Japanese?

CHLORINE
No he was English. When you put it on you can't hear a thing. If you like it, you can buy it off me for twenty quid. And you

know, everybody who sees this hat says to me...

CHLORINE
"WHERE DID YOU GET THAT HAT?
WHERE DID YOU GET THAT STYLE?
ISN'T IT A JOLLY ONE? IT DON'T 'ALF MAKE ME SMILE
I SHOULD LIKE TO HAVE ONE, JUST THE SAME AS THAT."
WHERE'ER I GO, THEY SHOUT
"HELLO! WHERE DID YOU GET THAT HAT?"

MAUREEN
Chlorine, there's nothing magic about that hat. You've been had.

CHLORINE
Not for years, dear, not for years.

MAUREEN
Only a stupid person would be interested in that hat.

CHLORINE
Do you want to try it?

MAUREEN
Go on then.

    Music in.

Where did you get it from anyway?

(_____) denotes when CHLORINE puts the hat on MAUREEN. During this, there is silence, until the music and vocals kick back in. It is as if the sound has been muted.

CHLORINE
Well...
ONE FINE DAY THE POLICE CAME ROUND WHILE I WAS COOKING LUNCHEON

_____WITH HIS
TRUNCHEON.
I SAID 'YOUNG MAN_____ PURE
CHEEK'
_____ SO INSTEAD WE USED A
LEAK.

MAUREEN:
OH WHERE DID YOU GET THAT HAT? WHERE DID YOU GET
THAT STYLE?
ALL:
ISN'T IT A JOLLY ONE? IT DON'T 'ALF MAKE ME SMILE
   (paying her)
MAUREEN:
I SHOULD LIKE TO HAVE ONE, JUST THE SAME AS THAT.
ALL:
WHERE'ER I/YOU GO, THEY'LL SHOUT "HELLO!
WHERE DID YOU GET THAT HAT?"

MAUREEN
That's fantastic!

> *MAUREEN puts the hat on as CHLORINE speaks, soon
> realising that she can hear everything.*

CHLORINE
I thought you might like it, Maureen, it's a pleasure doing
business with you.

MAUREEN
Eh wait a minute, I can hear everything. Give me back my
money.

CHLORINE
Sorry Maureen the deal's been done. But here comes Buttons,
see if you can fool him and get your money back.

> *BUTTONS enters.*

MAUREEN
Buttons, what are you doing here?

BUTTONS
I couldn't sleep so I got a last minute ticket to the Ball online.

MAUREEN
Buttons, if you can't sleep I have the answer to all your troubles. This is a magic hat. When you put it on you can't hear a thing. If you like it, you can buy it off me for twenty quid.

BUTTONS
Maureen, there's nothing magic about that hat. You've been had.

MAUREEN
Not for years, ducky, not for years.

BUTTONS
Only a stupid person would be interested in that.

MAUREEN
Do you want to try it?

BUTTONS
Go on then. Where did you get it from anyway?

MAUREEN
Well...
ONE DAY THE LOCAL BUTCHER CAME AND KNOCKED UPON MY COTTAGE.
_____ WITH HIS SAUSAGE.
I SAID 'YOUNG MAN_____ FR'A STARTER',
_____ TWO SPROUTS AND A CHIPOLATA.

BUTTONS:
OH WHERE DID YOU GET THAT HAT? WHERE DID YOU GET

70

THAT STYLE?
ALL:
ISN'T IT A JOLLY ONE? IT DON'T 'ALF MAKE ME SMILE
  (paying her)
BUTTONS:
I SHOULD LIKE TO HAVE ONE, JUST THE SAME AS THAT.
ALL:
WHERE'ER I/YOU GO, THEY'LL SHOUT "HELLO!
WHERE DID YOU GET THAT HAT?"

> *BUTTONS puts the hat on as MAUREEN speaks, soon*
> *realising that she can hear everything.*

That is awesome!

MAUREEN
I thought you might like it, Buttons, it's a pleasure doing
business with you.

BUTTONS
Eh wait a minute, I can hear everything. Give me back my
money.

MAUREEN
Sorry, Buttons, the deal's been done. But look, here comes
the equerry, see if you can fool him.

CHLORINE
But this time, let's not give the game away.

> *DANDINI enters.*

BUTTONS
Hello there I'm Buttons, what's your name?

DANDINI
Dandini.

BUTTONS
Dandelion?

DANDINI
Dandini!

BUTTONS
Dandoodoo?

DANDINI
Dandini!!

BUTTONS
Asparagus?

DANDINI
Stop it!

BUTTONS
Sorry it must be the noise from the party.

DANDINI
It is very loud, I'll give you that.

BUTTONS
Ah then what you need is this magic hat. When you put it on you can't hear a thing.

DANDINI
A magic hat?

BUTTONS
Yes I'll let you try it, and if you like it, you can buy it off us for twenty quid.

Well...
THIS WEEK INSTEAD OF HEALTHY FOOD I'M EATING JUST BAKED BEANS

_____ WHAT IT MEANS.

BUT *(**UGLIES**: 'OH MY GOD')*_____ A PONG.
_____ IT STAYS AROUND QUITE LONG.

DANDINI:
OH WHERE DID YOU GET THAT HAT? WHERE DID YOU GET
THAT STYLE?
ALL:
ISN'T IT A JOLLY ONE? IT DON'T 'ALF MAKE ME SMILE
   (NOT paying him)
DANDINI:
I SHOULD LIKE TO HAVE ONE, JUST THE SAME AS THAT.
ALL:
WHERE'ER I/YOU GO, THEY'LL SHOUT "HELLO!
WHERE DID YOU GET THAT HAT?"

Everybody!

   At various points, Dandini tries the hat on.

ALL:
WHERE DID YOU GET THAT HAT? WHERE DID YOU GET THAT
STYLE?
_____IT DON'T 'ALF MAKE ME SMILE
I SHOULD LIKE TO HAVE ONE, _____ THAT
WHERE'ER I GO, THEY'LL SHOUT "_____"
_____ DID _____ GET _____ HAT?"

   DANDINI puts the hat on.

DANDINI
Wow that really is a magic hat. Thank you so much!

BUTTONS
(Hand out)

A pleasure doing business with you good sir, that'll be twenty squid please... twenty of your finest smacaroons... Mate you owe me twenty pounds!

DANDINI
Sorry, can't hear a thing with this hat on.

DANDINI exits. **Tag***. All exit.*

Scene 3 - The Royal Ballroom (full stage)

FAIRY LIQUID and the ENSEMBLE are partying

SONG pop medley
(ENSEMBLE, FAIRY LIQUID AND BUTTONS)

FAIRY LIQUID
Ladies and gents, boys and girls, it's time for the Royal Ball's Royal Cabaret. And I am your host, Fairy Liquid.

Song 1:
(FAIRY LIQUID)

Ladies and Gentlemen, it's the man you've all been waiting for, back by public transport, it's Buttons!

BUTTONS enters.

SONG 2:
(FAIRY LIQUID & BUTTONS)

BUTTONS
Thanks kids, thank you. I've got another gig in [Romford] so I'll be back in a bit.

Tag, as FAIRY LIQUID and BUTTONS exit.

DANDINI
(Entering)
Ladies and Gentlemen, please take your partners for the Grand Waltz.

CINDERELLA and PRINCE CHARMING re-enter and dance in the centre.

Song: Grand Waltz

SFX: The clock strikes twelve.

CINDERELLA
Oh no!

PRINCE CHARMING
Princess Crystal, what's the matter?

CINDERELLA
I have to leave.

She heads up the stairs

PRINCE CHARMING
But you can't you've only just arrived.

CINDERELLA
I must, I'm sorry. I wish I could stay. Please don't try to stop me.

CINDERELLA exits.

PRINCE CHARMING
Princess Crystal, wait! Dandini, go after her!

DANDINI rushes up the stairs. A DOUBLE of Cinderella rushes across dressed as a scullery maid.

DANDINI
She's gone your highness, there was no one there but a scullery maid.

PRINCE CHARMING
How can she just disappear like that? Are you sure there's no sign of her?

DANDINI

None at all sir. But look at this. She seems to have left her crystal slipper behind.

PRINCE CHARMING
(Taking the slipper)
Her crystal slipper? In that case I have a proclamation.

> *Fanfare. Music in. Everyone gathers around immediately.*

Let it be known, that whomsoever's foot the crystal slipper fits, I shall ask her to be my bride. May a search of the entire land be organised *immediately*!

SONG Heroic Ballad
   (Prince charming)

> *Cloth in.*

Scene 4 - Edge of the Forest (front cloth)

BUTTONS and FAIRY LIQUID enters

BUTTONS
> My name's buttons **(doo doo doo doo doo)**

MAUREEN and CHLORINE enter.
MAUREEN with chips, CHLORINE with lambrini.

Ladies, come and meet my new friend, Fairy Liquid. We sang together at the party.

FAIRY LIQUID
Hi girls.

MAUREEN
Y'alright love?

BUTTONS
Say hello Chlorine.

CHLORINE
Hello Chlorine.

MAUREEN
That was the best buffet I have ever had. And I always thought that Coq au Vin meant love in a lorry.

FAIRY LIQUID
I think I ate too many kinder eggs.

CHLORINE
You're full of surprises. I was offered a tongue sandwich but I won't eat anything that comes from a cows mouth.

BUTTONS

What did you have then?

CHLORINE
Just a boiled egg.

MAUREEN
Do you not like Scampi?

CHLORINE
I like *all* Disney films.

BUTTONS
I had the Beef Stew Beef Stew.

FAIRY LIQUID
Beef Stew Beef Stew?

BUTTONS
It keeps repeating on me. Yesterday I tried to change my e-mail password to 'Beef Stew', but it said it wasn't stroganoff. It said I needed a password eight characters long with at least one big character, so I chose Snow White and the Seven Dwarfs.

SFX of howls and rattles.

BUTTONS
What was that?!

MAUREEN
I don't like that sound.

CHLORINE
No it reminds me of Halloween, and there's one thing I don't like about Halloween.

BUTTONS

Which is?

CHLORINE
That's right.

FAIRY LIQUID
Can we sing a song to keep our spirits up?

BUTTONS
Good idea. We could do that Elton John song where he hates talking about Indian clothing.

FAIRY LIQUID
What's that?

BUTTONS
Sari seems to be the hardest word.

FAIRY LIQUID
I could play Dancing Queen on the didgeridoo.

MAUREEN
That would be Abbariginal.

CHLORINE
Is there anything by *The Doors*?

BUTTONS
Yes there's a steward and a fire extinguisher.

CHLORINE
I know, why don't we sing 'Y Viva España'?

FAIRY LIQUID
That's a brilliant idea.

MAUREEN

And we can pretend we're in sunny Spain.

CHLORINE
Very good. Start us off Uncle Joe. One, two, three.

> *Music. The band play but the music is decidedly limp
> and slow, soon to be stopped by CHLORINE.*

Hang on a minute, hang on Uncle Joe. We don't want it like
that.

BUTTONS
No we need it much more upbeat, like erm *(big singing and
AIR-matadoring)* Da duduh duh,

ALL
> *(continuing together)*
- da da da duduh

CHLORINE
Yes that's much better. Can you and the chaps do that for us?
Excellent, okay, I'll count you in: one, two, three!

BAND
> *(An accurate verbal impression, with actions - no music
> playing)*
Da duduh duh, da da da duduh

CHLORINE
> *(to audience)*
Don't encourage them! I don't get paid enough for this.

MAUREEN
You're getting paid?

SONG: Y *Viva España 1a* w/verse and intro
> (UGLIES, FAIRY & BUTTONS)
*Rights must be obtained separately for use of this song

Meanwhile... BUTTONS and FAIRY dance in the centre.
MAUREEN and CHLORINE dance off to the sides.
CHLORINE returns in a sombrero holding a Sangria.
MAUREEN returns in sombrero and moustache.

MAUREEN
It's a lovely song, Chlorine, but I still feel frightened.

FAIRY LIQUID
Me too.

BUTTONS
Me three.

CHLORINE
Well I tell you what: boys and girls, if you see anything untoward, will you shout as loudly as you can and tell us? **(Yes)** Will you? **(Yes!).** Brilliant! Right we'll come straight in this time - after four Uncle Joe: one two four.

SONG: Y *Viva España*[1] *2a (no intro)*

Meanwhile... as they sing, a mummy comes on and dances behind them.

CHLORINE and MAUREEN head off to the sides.
MAUREEN returns with giant sunglasses and a cigar,
CHLORINE returns with a large Spanish flag wrapped around her, and a fan (in addition to the already gathered props).

ALL
Did something happen? **(Yes)** What was it? **(A Mummy)** Where was it? **(Behind you)** Behind us?!

---

[1] A licence issued to perform this play does not include permission to use the music specified in this copy.

CHLORINE
Right, Buttons and Fairy Liquid, you better go into the
audience and have a look too.

*BUTTONS goes up to the balcony. FAIRY LIQUID goes down
into the stalls.*

MAUREEN
We'll have to sing it again then but this time you need to
shout -

CHLORINE & MAUREEN
- much, much louder!

CHLORINE
After four Uncle Joe: one twelve four.

SONG: Y *Viva España 2b (no intro)*

> *Meanwhile... As they sing a MUMMY dances around
> them and many more MUMMIES go into the
> auditorium. One MUMMY chases FAIRY LIQUID out of
> the auditorium.*

> *CHLORINE and MAUREEN head off to the sides,
> MAUREEN returns with a ukulele, and CHLORINE
> returns with a piñata.*

CHLORINE
I think someone's run off with Fairy Liquid!

CHLORINE & MAUREEN
What was it? **(A mummy)** A mummy?! **(Yes!)**

MAUREEN
We'll have to sing it again then but this time you need to
shout -

CHLORINE & MAUREEN
- much, much louder!

CHLORINE
After four Uncle Joe: A hundred and twenty four.

SONG: Y *Viva España 2c (no intro)*

>*Meanwhile... As they sing a MUMMY dances around
>them and many more MUMMIES go into the
>auditorium. One MUMMY chases BUTTONS out of the
>auditorium.*

>*CHLORINE and MAUREEN head off to the sides,
>MAUREEN returns with an inflatable cactus, and
>CHLORINE returns with two tap dancers.*

MAUREEN
What have they got to do with Spain?

CHLORINE
These, Señora, are the tapas. And this one, he has a rubber
toe. We call him:

CHLORINE & MAUREEN & tapper
Roberto!

>*The TAP DANCERS exit.*

CHLORINE
(Suddenly noticing)
I think someone's run off with Buttons!

CHLORINE & MAUREEN
What was it? **(A mummy)** A mummy?! **(Yes!)**

MAUREEN
Oh I'm really scared now.

CHLORINE
I know, let's sing it again but so that we don't attract the mummies, let's sing it very, very quietly. After four Uncle Joe: Ready steady FOUR!

SONG: Y *Viva España 2d (no intro)*

> *Meanwhile... As they sing, MUMMIES invade the auditorium and the stage. Eventually all the MUMMIES are onstage, dancing next to CHLORINE and MAUREEN in a salsa line holding maracas. CHLORINE and MAUREEN are still laden with props.*
>
> *Eventually the music stops. The UGLIES look to each other, to the mummies, go to scream, but the MUMMIES scream first and run off.*

CHLORINE & MAUREEN
Charming!

> *Playout. MAUREEN and CHLORINE chase them off.*
>
> *Cloth out.*

Scene 5 - The Kitchen (full stage)

CINDERS is cleaning happily. BUTTONS rushes in.

BUTTONS
Cinders, there you are.

CINDERELLA
Morning, Buttons.

BUTTONS
I'm so sorry you missed out last night, Cinders. I managed to get into the Royal Palace. It turns out the Prince's balls are even more magnificent than we thought.

CINDERELLA
There's no need to be sorry, Buttons, I was there too.

BUTTONS
You were there too? Don't tell me you're madly in love with Dandini.

CINDERELLA
No, quite the opposite.

BUTTONS
Oh brilliant. I'm so relieved. Because I need to tell you that I love you.

CINDERELLA
And I love you too Buttons.

BUTTONS
You do!?

CINDERELLA
As a friend.

BUTTONS
As a friend?

CINDERELLA
It wasn't Dandini I met after all, it was the Prince. And I am in
love with the Prince.

BUTTONS
The Prince?

CINDERELLA
He's kind!

BUTTONS
I'm kind.

CINDERELLA
Funny.

BUTTONS
I'm funny.

CINDERELLA
Sexy

BUTTONS
I'm kind.

CINDERELLA
Please don't be upset Buttons. You know you'll always be my
best friend.

BUTTONS
    (pointing off)
Sexy Prince Boyfriend.
    (pointing at himself.)
Ugly Buttons Bestfriend.

CINDERELLA
Buttons you are not ugly! You're just not my type.

BUTTONS
(Sunglasses on. Full diva whilst slowly exiting)
I love my curves, my imperfections and my jiggling thighs. No
one said you had to.

CINDERELLA
Buttons?

BUTTONS
Go find someone else to feed your ego - I'm busy...

CINDERELLA
Buttons?

BUTTONS
Some people are like clouds. When they disappear, it's a
brighter day...

BUTTONS exits.

CHLORINE and MAUREEN enter.

CHLORINE
Cinderella, get out of here quick. We don't want you scaring
off the Prince. He's on his way to try the slipper on us.

CINDERELLA
He is?

MAUREEN
As we speak.

CINDERELLA
Then I shall stay and try it on too.

CHLORINE
Don't be ridiculous. The slipper was left at the Palace.

MAUREEN
Where the Prince holds his balls and dances.

CINDERELLA
I was at the Palace too.

CHLORINE
Don't be stupid.

CINDERELLA
And it was *my* slipper.

MAUREEN
Rubbish.

CINDERELLA
And here's the *other* one.

    UGLIES step back in amazement.

CHLORINE & MAUREEN
The other one!?

CINDERELLA
Yes.

CHLORINE & MAUREEN
You're Princess Crystal?!

CINDERELLA
Yes.

CHLORINE
Well... This *is* good news, Cinderella.

MAUREEN
Eh?

CHLORINE
I'm absolutely thrilled you're going to marry the Prince.

MAUREEN
I thought you'd be horrified.

> *CHLORINE elbows her. Cartoon loud SFX thud.*

CHLORINE
But you couldn't possibly meet the Prince in your rags. I know - I've a couple of new dresses you could try on down in the cellar. They're from Harrods.

MAUREEN
No they're not - they're from Asda.

> *CHLORINE elbows her. Cartoon loud SFX thud.*

CINDERELLA
Why are they in the cellar?

CHLORINE
It's so warm and cozy down there, and the lighting is perfect.

MAUREEN
Yesterday you described it as a prison cell.

> *CHLORINE full blown punches her.*
> *Cartoon loud SFX punch.*
> *MAUREEN flies off stage with the momentum.*

CHLORINE
Come on Cinders. You go first - I'll follow.

CINDERELLA
(To audience)
What do you think boys and girls? Shall I go down to the cellar? (**No!**)
(To Chlorine)
I better not. My friends are saying no.

CHLORINE
They're saying yes.

CINDERELLA
They're saying no.

CHLORINE
(to the Audience)
Are you saying no? **(Yes)** See they're saying yes.

CINDERELLA
No I think they meant -

CHLORINE
(Pushing her in)
Oh just get in there! That door locks itself and is totally sound proofed. She can scream at the top of her lungs and no one will ever hear her.

SFX Doorbell. MAUREEN re-enters.

MAUREEN
The Prince!

CHLORINE
The Prince!

BUTTONS
(entering)
The knobbly Prince is here.

CHLORINE
Don't you mean the noble Prince?

BUTTONS
You've not seen the tights he's wearing.

> Short fanfare.
> DANDINI and PRINCE CHARMING enter.
> DANDINI carries a cushion with the slipper on it.

PRINCE CHARMING
Good morning. Are your ladies here, ready and willing?

BUTTONS
I'm afraid not, Ready and Willing moved out last month. Now, who are you?

PRINCE CHARMING
I am Prince Charming.

BUTTONS
> (Macho, on tip toes)
Oh! Prince Charming hey? The sexy prince?

PRINCE CHARMING
Famous for his balls yes.

BUTTONS
How do you *do*?

PRINCE CHARMING
How do you do.

BUTTONS
> (To Dandini)
How do *you* do?

DANDINI
How do you do too.

BUTTONS
How do you two do too?

DANDINI & PRINCE CHARMING
How do you do too.

BUTTONS
    (to the wings)
How do you do R2D2?

        A toy R2D2 appears at the side. It beeps to the rhythm
        of 'How do you do too', then disappears.

PRINCE CHARMING
Let's get a move on, shall we?

CHLORINE
Alright Maureen, you go first. Give her a chair.

ALL
Hooray!

CHLORINE
A *chair* - not a cheer.

        BUTTONS puts a chair out.

MAUREEN
Your royal highknickers. I am an illegible maiden.

PRINCE CHARMING
Have you been chaste?

MAUREEN

All over [local town].

DANDINI tries to put the slipper on Maureen.

DANDINI
May I try it on?

MAUREEN
You can try it on anytime.

DANDINI
I'm afraid it's too tight.

MAUREEN
Try again with the tongue out.

DANDINI
        (With his tongue out)
I'm afraid it's too tight.

MAUREEN
I think my rather warm winter woolly socks are really rather in the way.

DANDINI
You can say that again.

MAUREEN
No I can't. Whip off m' socks will you.

> *DANDINI starts to take off MAUREEN's stocking. BUTTONS joins DANDINI as they try to pull the stocking off. The stocking is very long. General adlib, as Dandini exits off SL holding it, runs round the back and enters SR holding what looks like the far end of the sock. Eventually it comes off.*

DANDINI
It's no good. Your foot's too big anyway. You are not the Prince's love.

MAUREEN
		(Histrionically)
I'm overwrought! I'm overwhelmed! I'm overcome!

BUTTONS
You're overacting!

CHLORINE
Me next. Mind the verruca, won't you?

PRINCE CHARMING
Hurry up and try it on Dandini.

		DANDINI puts the slipper on CHLORINE.

BUTTONS
If it fits Dandini, that would be a surprise ending.

DANDINI
It fits!

ALL
It fits?!

CHLORINE
It fits! Book the church, buy a hat, put an announcement in [local newspaper]! It's on, it's on!

		DANDINI pulls off a false leg.

DANDINI
It's off, it's off.

BUTTONS
Chlorine, you're legless again.

CHLORINE
That was the leg I was wearing last night.

DANDINI
It doesn't fit and you haven't a leg to stand on.

PRINCE CHARMING
I've had enough of this. Are there no other eligible ladies in the house?

MAUREEN
There's a beautiful young lady called Cinder -

>CHLORINE *punches her. Cartoon SFX punch.*
>*She flies offstage the same as before.*

>BUTTONS *goes to speak.*

PRINCE CHARMING
Well Buttons?

CHLORINE
Buttons won't say a word, or the girl he loves will be lost forever.

BUTTONS
Your highness. The girl you're looking for is Cinderella. She deserves to be happy more than anyone I know, but I don't know where she is.(*To the audience*) Do you know where she is boys and girls? **(She's been locked in the cellar).** She's been locked in the cellar? Where? Over there?!

>DANDINI *rushes to open it.*

DANDINI

It's locked.

CHLORINE
What a pity.

PRINCE CHARMING
Arrest that woman!

*DANDINI, and MAUREEN (re-entering), grab
CHLORINE. PRINCE CHARMING rushes to the cellar.*

CHLORINE
Maureen, how could you!

MAUREEN
I'm sorry Chlorine. But I look at your firm face and I think
you're not half the man I am.

PRINCE CHARMING
We'll have to take the door off somehow. Buttons, is there a
B&Q in [Chelmsford]?

BUTTONS
No but there's a C, an H, an E, an L, an -

FAIRY LIQUID enters.

Hold it, folks, I'm Fairy Liquid,
A friend of Cinderella.
Our friends are right - old Chlorine's locked,
Poor Cinders in the cellar.

But though I'm watching over her
I cannot set her free,
The question that we need to ask is:
Who's got the key? (*Nigel:* **I've got the key, I've got the
key!**)

BUTTONS
[Nigel]'s got the key! Well done [Nigel]!

> *BUTTONS runs into the audience to get the key off [Nigel] and hands it to PRINCE CHARMING who runs to unlock the cellar. In the meantime BUTTONS takes Nigel through the pass door to the wings.*

CHLORINE
Nigel how could you? Don't you want to kiss me under the mistletoe... What do you mean you wouldn't kiss me under anaesthetic!

CINDERELLA
> *(entering)*

I'm free!

ALL
> *(off)*

She's free!

CINDERELLA
Prince Charming!

> *CINDERELLA runs into PRINCE CHARMING arms.*

ALL
Hooray!

BUTTONS
Quickly - try on the slipper!

PRINCE CHARMING
> *(Trying on the slipper)*

Princess Crystal!

CINDERELLA
Cinderella, actually.

PRINCE CHARMING
Cinderella. It fits!

ALL
Hooray!

MAUREEN
What shall we do with my wicked-ugly-older-twin sister?

CINDERELLA
What shall we do with her boys and girls? **(response)**

BUTTONS
Kill her? We can't kill her it's a pantomime!

FAIRY LIQUID
What do *you* think, Cinderella?

CINDERELLA
			(Handing her a bucket)
Well Chlorine, I forgive you - but not until you've scrubbed
the walls, the floors, the windows and doors -

MAUREEN
And all my dirty crevices!

CHLORINE
			(running off, away from MAUREEN)
Noooo!

PRINCE CHARMING
We must all gather together and honour our hero! Bring
fourth our hero!

			BUTTONS brings [NIGEL] onstage. All the ENSEMBLE
			enter too, one carrying a decorative box/podium,
			which Nigel stands on. A pink (hen party) sash is
			placed on him, with the words '[NIGEL] of

[Chelmsford]'.

Nigel of [Chelmsford], you will be remembered forever here in [Essex]. With great legends, like [Dame Maggie Smith]! And [Gemma Collins]! You have brought this land great happiness, and for this we say:

SONG: THANK YOU [NIGEL] A.K.A Rule Britannia
(Starting from the lyric 'This was the charter')

ALL
[NIGEL] OF [CHELMSFORD], YOU'VE GIVEN US THE KEY.
OUR LIVES FOREVER SHALL BE FREE.

THANK YOU [NIGEL], FOR GIVING US THE KEY.
CHELMSFORD ALWAYS AND FOREVER SHALL BE FREE.

THANK YOU [NIGEL], FOR GIVING US THE KEY.
CHELMSFORD ALWAYS AND FOREVER SHALL BE FREE.

> *(They all turn, with [Nigel], to DANDINI who takes a Polaroid photo.)*

> *Music ends. Short **tag** immediately.*

DANDINI
> *(Escorting NIGEL off, over tag, giving him a photo)*
'Nigel of Chelmsford' everyone.

BUTTONS
Oh wow, isn't this brilliant! Cinderella's found Princey and Maureen's clearly going to go home with [Nigel], *(Starting to cry)* I love it when my best friends are in a relationship **(Aah)**.

CINDERELLA
> *(Whisper)*

Buttons you're not the only single person here, what about
        (nodding towards Fairy Liquid, mm-ing 'Fairy Liquid')
Mm-m-m-m?

BUTTONS
Mm-m-m-m? She'd never go for me.

CINDERELLA
If you don't ask you'll never know.

        *Everyone mutters words of encouragement. He kneels
        down nervously in front of Fairy Liquid.*

BUTTONS
Fairy Liquid?

FAIRY LIQUID
Yes Buttons?

        He clears his throat, this is the real deal.

BUTTONS
The sky is blue when it greets the sun
The stars are bright when the day is done.
Orangutans are Southeast Asian.
But I'm not a poet. Kiss me!

ALL
Buttons!

FAIRY LIQUID
You're not the best at flirting Buttons
And you're poems aren't too good,
But now's not the time, for speaking in rhyme
Because I really fancy you so why the heck not?

ALL
Hooray!

She kisses him. PRINCE CHARMING gets down on one knee.

PRINCE CHARMING
There's still one question that remains, Cinderella, will you marry me?

CINDERELLA
Oh yes I will!

SONG Happy Ever After
   (Full company except Chlorine)

Tag. *Cloth in.*

Scene 6 - Songsheet (front cloth)

SONG: The Animals Have Escaped
(to the tune of Boiled beef and carrots)

BUTTONS
My name's buttons **(doo doo doo doo doo)**
My name's buttons **(doo doo doo doo doo)**
My name's buttons **(doo doo doo doo doo)**
My name's buttons

Hiya everybody, are you having a good time? (**Yes**). Do you all wanna come to the wedding? (**Yes**). Shall we have a sing song? (**Yes**).

Music in.

Excellent, well let me tell you a little story about when I was your age and I went on a bit of a day out...

WHEN I WAS ONLY 4 YEARS OLD
MY MOTHER AND MY FATHER, TOO
THEY DIDN'T KNOW WHAT TO DO WITH ME
SO THEY TOOK ME TO THE ZOO.
BUT WHEN WE GOT THERE TO THE ZOO
THERE WERE PEOPLE RUNNING WILD
AND THE KEEPER SHOUTED OUT TO US
LIKE A VERY EXCITED CHILD:

THE...
SPIDERS HAVE ESCAPED. THE SPIDERS HAVE ESCAPED.
TICKLING HERE, TICKLING THERE, TICKLING SOMEONE ELSE'S HAIR
I DON'T KNOW WHERE THEY ARE BUT I DO KNOW THEY HAVE ESCAPED
IT'LL BE ALL RIGHT SO PLEASE DON'T FRIGHT.
BUT OOPS THEY HAVE ESCAPED.

Come on everyone, join in and do the actions with me.

THE SPIDERS HAVE ESCAPED. THE SPIDERS HAVE ESCAPED.
TICKLING HERE, TICKLING THERE, TICKLING SOMEONE
ELSE'S HAIR
I DON'T KNOW WHERE THEY ARE BUT I DO KNOW THEY
HAVE ESCAPED
IT'LL BE ALL RIGHT SO PLEASE DON'T FRIGHT.
BUT OOPS THEY HAVE ESCAPED.

WHEN I WAS ONLY 5 YEARS OLD
MY MOTHER AND MY FATHER, TOO
THEY DIDN'T KNOW WHAT TO DO WITH ME
SO THEY TOOK ME TO THE ZOO.
BUT WHEN WE GOT THERE TO THE ZOO
THERE WERE PEOPLE RUNNING WILD
AND THE KEEPER SHOUTED OUT TO US
LIKE A VERY EXCITED CHILD:

THE SPIDERS AND THE...

WORMS THEY HAVE ESCAPED, THE WORMS THEY HAVE
ESCAPED,
WIGGLING UP, WIGGLING DOWN, WIGGLING-WIGGLING ALL
AROUND
TICKLING HERE, TICKLING THERE, TICKLING SOMEONE
ELSE'S HAIR
I DON'T KNOW WHERE THEY ARE BUT I DO KNOW THEY
HAVE ESCAPED
IT'LL BE ALL RIGHT SO PLEASE DON'T FRIGHT.
BUT OOPS THEY HAVE ESCAPED.

WHEN I WAS ONLY 6 YEARS OLD
MY MOTHER AND MY FATHER, TOO
THEY DIDN'T KNOW WHAT TO DO WITH ME
SO THEY TOOK ME TO THE ZOO.
BUT WHEN WE GOT THERE TO THE ZOO
THERE WERE PEOPLE RUNNING WILD

AND THE KEEPER SHOUTED OUT TO US
LIKE A VERY EXCITED CHILD:

THE SPIDERS AND THE WORMS AND THE...

DUCKS HAVE ESCAPED. THE DUCKS THEY HAVE ESCAPED.
WADDLING LEFT, WADDLING RIGHT, SOMETIMES WADDLING
LEFT *AND* RIGHT
WIGGLING UP, WIGGLING DOWN, WIGGLING-WIGGLING ALL
AROUND
TICKLING HERE, TICKLING THERE, TICKLING SOMEONE
ELSE'S HAIR
I DON'T KNOW WHERE THEY ARE BUT I DO KNOW THEY
HAVE ESCAPED
IT'LL BE ALL RIGHT SO PLEASE DON'T FRIGHT.
BUT OOPS THEY HAVE ESCAPED.

WHEN I WAS ONLY 7 YEARS OLD
MY MOTHER AND MY FATHER, TOO
THEY DIDN'T KNOW WHAT TO DO WITH ME
SO THEY TOOK ME TO THE ZOO.
BUT WHEN WE GOT THERE TO THE ZOO
THERE WERE PEOPLE RUNNING WILD
AND THE KEEPER SHOUTED OUT TO US
LIKE A VERY EXCITED CHILD:

THE SPIDERS AND THE WORMS AND THE DUCKS AND THE...

KANGAROOS HAVE ESCAPED. THE KANGAROOS HAVE
ESCAPED.
JUMPING HIGH, JUMPING LOW, JUMPING EVERYWHERE THEY
GO
WADDLING LEFT, WADDLING RIGHT, SOMETIMES WADDLING
LEFT *AND* RIGHT
WIGGLING UP, WIGGLING DOWN, WIGGLING-WIGGLING ALL
AROUND
TICKLING HERE, TICKLING THERE, TICKLING SOMEONE
ELSE'S HAIR

I DON'T KNOW WHERE THEY ARE BUT I DO KNOW THEY
HAVE ESCAPED
IT'LL BE ALL RIGHT SO PLEASE DON'T FRIGHT.
BUT OOPS THEY HAVE ESCAPED.

WHEN I WAS ONLY 8 YEARS OLD
MY MOTHER AND MY FATHER, TOO
THEY DIDN'T KNOW WHAT TO DO WITH ME
SO THEY TOOK ME TO THE ZOO.
BUT WHEN WE GOT THERE TO THE ZOO
THERE WERE PEOPLE RUNNING WILD
AND THE KEEPER SHOUTED OUT TO US
LIKE A VERY EXCITED CHILD:

THE SPIDERS AND THE WORMS AND THE DUCKS AND THE
KANGAROOS AND THE...

ELEPHANTS HAVE ESCAPED. THE ELEPHANTS HAVE ESCAPED.
STOMPING BIG, STOMPING LOUD, STOMPING WILDLY
THROUGH THE CROWD
JUMPING HIGH, JUMPING LOW, JUMPING EVERYWHERE THEY
GO
WADDLING LEFT, WADDLING RIGHT, SOMETIMES WADDLING
LEFT *AND* RIGHT
WIGGLING UP, WIGGLING DOWN, WIGGLING-WIGGLING ALL
AROUND
TICKLING HERE, TICKLING THERE, TICKLING SOMEONE
ELSE'S HAIR
I DON'T KNOW WHERE THEY ARE BUT I DO KNOW THEY
HAVE ESCAPED
IT'LL BE ALL RIGHT SO PLEASE DON'T FRIGHT.
BUT OOPS THEY HAVE ESCAPED.

WHEN I WAS ONLY 9 YEARS OLD
MY MOTHER AND MY FATHER, TOO
THEY DIDN'T KNOW WHAT TO DO WITH ME
SO THEY TOOK ME TO THE ZOO.
BUT WHEN WE GOT THERE TO THE ZOO

THERE WERE PEOPLE RUNNING WILD
AND THE KEEPER SHOUTED OUT TO US
LIKE A VERY EXCITED CHILD:

THE SPIDERS AND THE WORMS AND THE DUCKS AND THE
KANGAROOS AND THE ELEPHANTS AND THE...

CHEETAHS HAVE ESCAPED. THE CHEETAHS HAVE ESCAPED
    (Slow)
AS THEY'RE FAST, WE WON'T LAST, UNLESS WE ALL GO
TWICE AS FAST.
    (Fast)
STOMPING BIG, STOMPING LOUD, STOMPING WILDLY
THROUGH THE CROWD
JUMPING HIGH, JUMPING LOW, JUMPING EVERYWHERE THEY
GO
WADDLING LEFT, WADDLING RIGHT, SOMETIMES WADDLING
LEFT *AND* RIGHT
WIGGLING UP, WIGGLING DOWN, WIGGLING-WIGGLING ALL
AROUND
TICKLING HERE, TICKLING THERE, TICKLING SOMEONE
ELSE'S HAIR
I DON'T KNOW WHERE THEY ARE BUT I DO KNOW THEY
HAVE ESCAPED
IT'LL BE ALL RIGHT SO PLEASE DON'T FRIGHT.
BUT OOPS THEY HAVE ESCAPED.

BUTTONS
    (Over playout)
Give yourselves a round of applause - see you at the
wedding!

Scene 7 - The Royal Wedding (full stage)

Bleed through, gauze up.

SONG: Walkdown

Bows as follows:
ENSEMBLE
DANDINI
FAIRY LIQUID
MAUREEN & CHLORINE
BUTTONS

Drum roll.

DANDINI
Three cheers for the Prince and Princess. Hip hip **(Hooray)**,
Hip hip **(Hooray)**, Hip hip **(Hooray)**.

CINDERELLA & PRINCE come down.

Music ends.

FAIR LIQUID
Our pantomime is over

DANDINI
But when the curtain falls,

CINDERELLA
Our hero Nigel will still be famous.

PRINCE CHARMING
More famous than my balls.

CHLORINE

I've decided to be nicer now
- It's fun I must confess.

MAUREEN
But what about you, you've been a great crowd,
Have you enjoyed yourselves? **(Yes)**

CINDERELLA
Merry Christmas then to all of you
Have a wonderful new year.

BUTTONS
If you want another song, [Chelmsford],
Come on let's hear you cheer!

SONG: Megamix

SONG: Exit Music

Curtain.

Guy Unsworth
Writer

Guy grew up in Southport, Lancashire. After reading Industrial Economics at the University of Nottingham, he studied Theatre Directing at Mountview Academy of Theatre Arts.

Guy worked as Assistant and Associate Director on numerous productions in the West End and at the Royal Shakespeare Company before establishing himself as an international, award-winning theatre director and writer.

Guy was a co-bookwriter with Alain Boublil (LES MISÉRABLES, MISS SAIGON) for the 2012 revival of MARGUERITE, and devised the narrative for the West End hit COOL RIDER. In 2016, he was part of the team behind the 90th Birthday Celebrations for the Queen. Guy's stage play, based on the classic TV comedy SOME MOTHERS DO 'AVE 'EM begun its UK tour in February 2018 to huge critical acclaim.

Guy has directed, written or performed in over 20 pantomimes.

www.guyunsworth.com

Printed in Great Britain
by Amazon